Top Secret

Guided/Group Reading Notes

Blue Band

Contents

OXFORD

Introduction

Reading progression in Year 5/Primary 6

By Year 5/Primary 6 the majority of children are developing into confident, capable readers. The focus is on continuing to build their enjoyment, reading fluency and their engagement with reading. Encouraging children to read widely in order to develop personal preferences, critical appreciation and comprehension is central to helping them become enthusiastic readers. Humour, adventure, suspense and identification with interesting characters and intriguing information texts all help create books children look forward to reading. They can sustain independent reading for extended periods of time but chapters and non-fiction spreads offer natural 'break points' for readers who may still find long texts challenging to read. They also create hooks to motivate the reader to want to read further.

Year 5/P6 children recognize most common words on sight. The texts at **blue band** include polysyllabic and more complex topic-based vocabulary. Explicit work on vocabulary continues to be important for improving both reading and writing. Introducing new vocabulary within meaningful contexts helps to extend children's vocabulary range. A wide range of vocabulary, sentence structures and verb tenses are used. Language play (puns, homophones, homonyms, codes, jokes, onomatopoeic words, etc.) can be found in the texts. Expressive, descriptive and figurative language and vocabulary help create moods and emotions.

In the fiction books, storylines are more complex, involving subplots or parallel settings. For example, in the **Top Secret** cluster, the character stories move between the safe location of NICE headquarters to various locations around the world.

The non-fiction books, too, are increasingly complex. They raise interesting discussion opportunities as well as providing a wealth of fascinating material. For example, the factual information about secrets and spying raises some complex moral issues around when an action is 'right' and when it is 'wrong'.

The non-fiction books offer examples of a wide range of genres. There are opportunities to compare and contrast different opinions and viewpoints and to evaluate situations and arguments. Texts may contain a balance of fact and opinion, and encouraging children to distinguish between these helps them respond critically.

Visual literacy is supported through the range of visual 'genres' used in the books, for example, comic strips, photo sequences and diagrammatic 'animations'. At blue band, the ratio of text to illustration is greater, but the illustrations continue to provide additional information and interest for the reader, including opportunities to compare and contrast visual information and source materials. Photos and illustrations add to the content and level of reading challenge, rather than simply supporting the text. Visualization comprehension strategies and activities that encourage the reader to reflect on the visual images are suggested in these *Guided/Group Reading Notes*.

The character books

The character stories at blue band show the children working as a team for Dani Day, who has become senior scientist for the National Institute for the Conservation of Earth (NICE). The children's adventures take them all over the world. In some stories they also encounter, and have to outwit, a new villain – the Collector. The Collector has one goal – to own the biggest collection of snow globes in the world. Using advanced micro science, he shrinks and steals valuable objects. It is up to Team X to stop him. The Collector taunts the children with riddles and clues, and he also commands a new X-bot – the Master-bot. The children need ingenuity and creative thinking to get out of the tricky situations they find themselves in as they try to thwart the Collector. Luckily, they have a range of new micro-sized gadgets and X-crafts and the backup of Dani's scientific expertise to help them.

In the 'set-up' story, *Team X*, Max, Cat, Ant and Tiger visit Dani Day at NICE. To their horror, she asks them to return their special watches, that allow them to shrink to micro-size, and gives them to her new, adult, team. While her new agents struggle to respond to an emergency, the children are quick off the mark. In the icy wastes of Patagonia they have their first encounter with the Master-bot. Using their watches they manage to outwit the Master-bot. On returning to NICE they encounter their first message from the Collector and realize his link to the defeated Dr X. Dani accepts that the children can become her Team X and assist her in future missions.

In *Meteorite*, the children travel to California where a mysterious meteorite is being held for safe-keeping. It appears safely guarded but the children are not convinced. Little do they know just how cunning the Collector has been and how close to disaster they will come.

The character non-fiction book *Crack the Code* explores how top-secret messages have been passed on throughout history. It features a variety of codes and ciphers, as well as some famous ones.

Guided/Group reading

By Year 5/P6, guided/group reading sessions offer opportunities for children to read independently in a focused way and take part in group discussion to enhance understanding, personal response and an appreciation of the author's craft, rather than concentrating on rehearsing and applying reading cues – although there may be occasions when revisiting these is useful.

These *Guided/Group Reading Notes* provide support for each book in the cluster, along with suggestions for follow-up activities. Suggestions are given for three guided/group reading sessions for each book. However, at blue band, children may read much of the book independently and only undertake one or two guided reading sessions around the text. Although guided/group reading suggestions are given under each section of the notes, teachers will select which chapters/non-fiction sections they wish to use in reading sessions.

Speaking, listening and drama

Talk continues to be crucial to learning. At Year 5/P6, children still need plenty of opportunities to express their ideas through talk and drama and to listen to and watch the ideas of others. These processes are important for building reading engagement, personal response and understanding, and for rehearsing some writing possibilities. Suggestions for speaking, listening and drama are provided for every book. Within these *Guided/Group Reading Notes* the speaking and listening activities are linked to the reading assessment focuses.

Building comprehension

Understanding what we have read is at the heart of reading. To help readers become effective in comprehending a text these *Guided/Group Reading Notes* contain practical strategies to develop the following important aspects of comprehension:

- Previewing
- Predicting
- Activating and building prior knowledge
- Questioning
- Recalling
- Visualizing and other sensory responses
- Deducing, inferring and drawing conclusions
- Determining importance
- Synthesizing
- Empathizing
- Summarizing
- Personal response, including adopting a critical stance.

The research basis and rationale for focusing of these aspects of comprehension is given in the *Teaching Handbook* for Year 5/P6.

The Project X *Interactive* software for Years 5 and 6/P6 and 7 contains comprehension activities for every book. In addition, higher comprehension skills are developed through activities in the 'Explore' section.

Reading fluency

Reading fluency combines automatic word recognition and reading with pace and expression. Rereading, fluency and building comprehension are linked together in a complex interrelationship, where each supports the other. This is discussed more fully in the *Teaching Handbook* for Year 5/P6. Opportunities for children to read aloud are important in building fluency and reading aloud to children provides models of expressive fluent reading. Suggestions for purposeful and enjoyable oral reading and rereading/re-listening activities are given in the follow-up activities to these *Guided/Group Reading Notes* and in the notes for parents on the inside back cover of each book.

The Project X *Interactive* software allows individuals or small groups of children to listen to the texts. Listening to stories being read, and hearing the text in the non-fiction books, is particularly effective with EAL children.

Building vocabulary

Explicit work on enriching vocabulary is important in building reading fluency and comprehension. By Year 5/P6 children have a familiar core vocabulary and reading is the most important means by which children encounter new vocabulary. However, further work needs to be undertaken if newly encountered written words are to become part of the child's vocabulary repertoire. Suggestions for vocabulary work are included in these notes. The vocabulary chart on pages 10–11 shows some of the ambitious vocabulary introduced in each book, along with vocabulary linked by meaning. Reusing new words orally or in their own writing helps these words become integrated into the child's working vocabulary. The chart also indicates those words that can be used to support a structured spelling programme.

Developing a thematic approach

Helping children make links in their learning supports their development as learners. All the books in this cluster have a focus on the theme of **Top Secret**. A chart showing the cross-curricular potential of this theme and further reading suggestions are given in the *Teaching Handbook* for Year 5/P6, along with a rationale for using thematic approaches. Some suggestions for cross-curricular activities are also given in these *Guided/Group Reading Notes*, in the follow-up suggestions for each book.

In guided/group reading sessions, you will also want to encourage children to make links between the books in the cluster. Grouping books in a cluster allows readers to make links between characters, events, actions and information across the books. This enables readers to gradually build complex understandings of characters and information, to give reasons why things happen and how characters may change and develop. It can help them to recognize cause and effect. It helps children reflect on the skill of determining importance, as a minor incident or detail in one book may prove to have greater significance when considered across several books.

Note that in this cluster, it is advisable to read *Team X* before *Meteorite*.

In the **Top Secret** cluster, some of the suggested links that can be explored across the books include:

- discussing the moral dilemmas around keeping or breaking secrets **(Citizenship, PSHE)**
- using codes and other methods of communicating 'secretly'/securely **(Literacy)**
- setting up experiments to create invisible messages. **(Science)**

Reading into writing

The character books provide both models and inspiration to support children's writing. Brief suggestions for relevant, contextualized and interesting writing activities are given in the follow-up activities for each book. These include both short and longer writing opportunities. They cover a wide range of writing contexts so writers can develop an understanding of adapting their writing for different audiences and purposes.

The Project X *Interactive* software contains a 'Write and Respond' section for every book. This section contains a number of writing frames and activity sheets that pupils can write/type into directly, or print off, plus some suggestions for extended writing. In addition, there is a collection of 'clip art' assets from the character books that children can use in their writing.

The section on Reading Journals in the *Teaching Handbook* for Year 5/P6 contains a wealth of suggested activities that can be used with any text. You may also wish to draw on these during guided/group reading sessions.

Selecting follow-up activities

These *Guided/Group Reading Notes* give many ideas for follow-up activities. Some of these can be completed within the reading session. Some are longer activities that will need to be worked on over time. You should select those activities that are most appropriate for your pupils. It is not expected that you would complete all the suggested activities.

Home/school reading

Books used in a guided/group reading session can also be used in home/school reading programmes.

Before a guided/group reading session, the child could:
- read the first chapter or section of the book
- read a related book from the cluster to build background knowledge.

Following a guided/group reading session, the child could:
- reread the book at home to build reading confidence and fluency
- read the next chapter in a longer book
- read a related book from the cluster.

Advice for parents on supporting their child in reading at home is provided on the inside back cover of individual books. There is further advice for teachers concerning home/school reading partnerships in the *Teaching Handbook* for Year 5/P6.

Assessment

During guided/group reading, teachers make ongoing reading assessments of individuals and of the group. Reading targets are indicated for each book and you should assess against these.

Select just one or two targets at a time as the focus for the group. The same target can be appropriate for several literacy sessions or over several texts.

Speaking and listening targets and writing targets are also given for each book, as guided/group reading sessions support these other modes of communication. One possible speaking and listening target and one writing target are given, linked to the suggested follow-up activities. The many suggested oral and writing tasks give ample further opportunities for other aspects of speaking and listening and writing to be assessed.

Readers should be encouraged to self-assess and peer-assess against the target/s.

Further support for assessing pupils' progress is provided in the *Teaching Handbook* for Year 5/P6.

 Continuous reading objectives and ongoing assessment

The following objective will be supported in *every* guided/group reading session and is therefore a continuous focus for attention and assessment (AF2/6). This objective is not repeated in full in each set of notes, but as you listen to individual children discussing their reading you should undertake ongoing assessment, against this objective:

- Reflect on reading habits and preferences and plan personal reading goals **8.1**

Further objectives are provided as a focus within the notes for each book, as appropriate, from these strands:

- Understanding and interpreting texts *(Strand 7)*
- Engaging with and responding to texts *(Strand 8)*.

Specific spelling objectives are not given with each book but some spelling and vocabulary building opportunities are indicated in the sessions.

Correlation to the specific objectives within the Scottish, Welsh and Northern Ireland curricula are provided in the *Teaching Handbook* for Year 5/P6.

Recording assessment

The assessment chart for the **Top Secret** cluster is provided in the *Teaching Handbook* for Year 5/P6.

 Diagnostic assessment

If an individual child is failing to make good progress or has a specific problem with some aspect of reading you will want to undertake a more detailed assessment. In the *Teaching Handbook* for Year 5/P6 checklists for reading attitudes and behaviours are given to assist with this. There is also a running records sheet for Blue band, or you may wish to track back to the running record sheets for Grey band in the *Teaching Handbook* for Year 4/P5.

 Vocabulary chart

At Year 5/P6, children should:

- read most words independently and automatically
- spell words containing unstressed vowels
- know and use less common prefixes and suffixes, such as *im-*, *ir-*, *-cian*
- group and classify words according to their spelling patterns and their meanings.

NB Examples only are given in each category.

Team X	Less common prefixes/ suffixes	auto–: autopilot anti–: anticlockwise en–: endangered, encased
	Spelling pattern	ious: previous, precious, obvious, serious, amphibious, anxiously
	Ambitious vocabulary	persisted, reluctant, immediately, expression, emergency, disappointed, extinction, investigate, plummeted
	Vocabulary linked by meaning	Words about ability: clever, brilliant, genius

Meteorite	Words containing unstressed vowels/ spelling pattern	−cuit: circuit (further examples not in text: biscuit, circuitous)
	Less common prefixes/ suffixes	tele−: teleport anti−: anticlockwise
	Ambitious vocabulary	population, confidential, restricted, consequences, qualifications, synchronize
	Vocabulary linked by meaning	Words linked to 'security': steel doors, laser beams, keypad, motion sensors, pressure sensors, security cameras, guards
Crack the Code	Less common prefixes/ suffixes	un−: unlocking, unbreakable, unwound, unravelled, unfortunately de−: decode
	Spelling pattern	ph: cipher, pharaohs, alphabet
	Ambitious vocabulary	civilization, communication, intercepted, parchment, cryptic, confident
	Vocabulary linked by meaning	Types of code/cipher: scytale, Caesar cipher, hieroglyphs, substitution, Enigma, bilingual, PIN (Personal Identity Number)
The Secret Diary of Danny Glover	Words containing unstressed vowels/ consonants	whispering, debt, Everest, management, definitely, platinum
	Spelling pattern	ph: phone, catchphrase, morphed
	Ambitious vocabulary	money management, publishers, international, paparazzi, suspicious, allergic
	Vocabulary linked by meaning	Words linked to 'secrecy': secret, pretended, password, gone to ground, gone into hiding
The Spy's Secret Handbook	Words containing unstressed vowels/ consonants	similar, listening, handkerchief, receipts
	Spelling pattern	ion: suspicion, corruption, information
	Ambitious vocabulary	terrorism, corruption, recruited, suspicion, recruited, surveillance, equipment, information, transmitters, technology
	Vocabulary linked by meaning	identity, identical

Team X

BY TONY BRADMAN

About this book

Max, Cat, Ant and Tiger are horrified when Dani Day asks them to hand over their watches to four adult agents who will form her problem-solving team. Then Max and his friends shrink into action to help her out. With their mission successfully accomplished, Dani agrees that they should become the new 'Team X'.

Big themes: working as a team

Writing genres: narrative, short messages, fact files, email

You will need

- *Vocabulary bookmark* Photocopy Master 18, *Teaching Handbook* for Year 5/P6
- *What are they thinking, feeling, saying?* Photocopy Master 27, *Teaching Handbook* for Year 5/P6
- *X-bot compare and contrast* Photocopy Master 1, *Teaching Handbook* for Year 5/P6
- *NICE 'Mission Accomplished' report* Photocopy Master 2, *Teaching Handbook* for Year 5/P6

	Literacy Framework objective	Target and assessment focus
Speaking, listening, group interaction and drama	○ Tell a story using notes designed to cue techniques, such as repetition, recap and humour **1.1**	○ We can retell a story from one character's point of view **AF2**
Reading	○ Make notes on and use evidence from across a text to explain events or ideas **7.1**	○ We can track ideas and information across the story **AF2**
	○ Explore how writers use language for comic and dramatic effects **7.5**	○ We can recognize and discuss how the author makes the story dramatic **AF5/6**
Writing	○ Experiment with different narrative forms and styles to write their own stories **9.2**	○ We can write a story from one character's point of view **AF1/2**

The following notes provide a structure for up to three guided/group reading sessions. They can be used flexibly; you can focus on all three sessions, two or one session. The rest of the book can be read independently by the children between sessions.

Select appropriate activities from the suggestions below depending on whether the children will read during the session or whether they have read prior to the session. In this instance you will skip the 'During reading' section, although, you may wish to include the 'As you read' activity as part of your discussion of what they have read independently. In Session 1, children will read to the end of Chapter 2. Prior to Session 2, ensure they have read Chapters 3–4 independently. In Session 2, they will read Chapters 5–6. Prior to Session 3, ensure they have read Chapter 7. In Session 3, they will read Chapters 8–9.

Session 1 (Chapters 1–2)

 Before reading

To activate prior knowledge and encourage prediction

- Look at pages 2–4 of the story. Ask the children to tell you what they already know about Max, Cat, Ant, Tiger, Dani Day and the watches. If this is their first encounter with the characters, check they understand the background story. **(activating prior knowledge)**
- Read page 5 to the children. What might Dani have in store for Max and his friends? **(predicting)**
- Before children read independently, ask them to rehearse what they might do if they become stuck on a word or sentence. The range of possible strategies (such as rereading, reading on, using context, using phonic, syntactic and vocabulary knowledge) should be well established for most readers and only an occasional reminder should be necessary.

 During reading

- Ask the children to read Chapters 1 and 2.
- Stress the importance of comprehension, reminding the children to stop and take action if they are failing to understand the text, e.g. by checking the meaning of a particular word or phrase, rereading more carefully, reading on to see if the meaning becomes clear, reading it aloud, discussing the passage with someone, etc.

- As they read, ask the children to note any new or unusual words, recording these on their *Vocabulary bookmark* Photocopy Master.

. . . . >

Assessment point

Listen to individual children reading and make ongoing assessments on their approaches to tackling new words, their reading fluency and their understanding of the text. **AF1**

 After reading

Returning to the text

- Ask the children:
  o What surprise announcement does Dani make when she meets Max, Cat, Ant and Tiger? **(recall)**
  o What four X-crafts do the friends see? **(recall)**
  o What reasons do Dani and the agents give for the children not being in Team X? **(recall)**

  Extension question: How do the children feel about handing over their watches? Why do you think Max hands his watch over and persuades the others to do so? **(deducing, inferring and drawing conclusions)**

The author's craft

- How does the author make the agents seem not very nice? Which words give this impression?

. . . . >

Assessment point

Can the children recognize how the author uses certain words to help shape our response to characters? **AF5/6**

Building comprehension

- Role play the scene on page 14 in which Dani asks for the watches and Max talks the others round. Freeze frame the scene at the point at which Dani passes the watches to the agents. Ask each character to say what they are thinking and feeling at that point. **(personal response, empathizing)**
- Ask the children to complete the grid on the *What are they thinking, feeling, saying?* Photocopy Master for one of the characters at that point in the story. **(adopting a critical stance, empathizing)**

Building vocabulary

- Share the words the children have recorded on their bookmarks and check that they understand their meaning.
- Prior to Session 2, ensure the children have read Chapters 3 and 4 independently.

Session 2 (Chapters 5–6)

 Before reading

To review previously read text

- Ask the children to briefly recap the story to date. **(recall)**

To encourage prediction

- Look at the title of Chapter 5 and invite the children to predict what the characters are going to do. **(predicting)**
- Before children read independently, ask them to rehearse what to do if they become stuck on a word or sentence.

 During reading

- Ask the children to read Chapters 5 and 6.
- Stress the importance of comprehension, reminding the children to stop and take action if they are failing to understand the text.
- As they read, ask them to notice the functions of the watches and the different skills the children use on Hawkwing.

. . . . >

Assessment point
Listen to individual children reading and make ongoing assessments on their approaches to tackling new words, their reading fluency and their understanding of the text. **AF1**

 After reading

Returning to the text

- Ask the children:
  - Why do the watches only work for the children? **(recall)**
  - Why does Max suggest they go to Patagonia? **(deducing, inferring and drawing conclusions)**
  - What is the Master-bot carrying? **(recall, deducing, inferring and drawing conclusions)**
  - **Extension question:** How do they think the friends will save the whales? **(predicting)**

The author's craft

- How does the author indicate the different emotions the children are feeling?

Building comprehension

- Looking at pictures from earlier books compare this new X-bot with X1, X2 and X3 bots, using the *X-bot compare and contrast* Photocopy Master to do this.

· ·>

- Prior to Session 3, ensure the children have read Chapter 7 independently.

Assessment point

Can the children track ideas and information from across the books? AF2

Session 3 (Chapters 8–9)

Before reading

To review previously read text

- Ask the children to tell you what happened in Chapter 7. **(recall)**

To support engagement with the text and reading fluency

- Read pages 37 and 38 aloud up to "You'd better tell me everything". Model Dani's different emotions through your voice. Ask the children to listen for how you are using your voice to bring the story to life.

- Before children read independently, ask them to rehearse what to do if they become stuck on a word or sentence.

During reading

- Ask the children to read Chapters 8 and 9.

- Stress the importance of comprehension, reminding the children to stop and take action if they are failing to understand the text.

- As they read, ask them to reflect on their personal feelings about the story.

· ·>

Assessment point

Listen to pairs of children reading to each other and make ongoing assessments on their reading fluency. AF1

After reading

Returning to the text

- Ask the children which sections they particularly liked/didn't like. **(personal response, including adopting a critical stance)**

16

Building comprehension

- What does the picture on page 39 tell us that isn't in the text? **(deducing, inferring and drawing conclusions)**

Ⓦ Make notes on what happens to the agents throughout the story. Using these notes, ask the children to retell/write the story from the point of view of one of the agents. Give them the ending
'When we finally got to the Research Station we found it had all been for nothing. Those missing whales were back. Work for Dani Day? Forget it! I quit.'

· ·➤

Assessment point

Can the children retell/write the story from a character's viewpoint? **AF1/2**

The author's craft

- Discuss places in the story where the author has put in an unexpected twist. What effect does this have on the reader? e.g. Dani taking the watches away; agents having different reactions to the watches; new X-bot appearing.

· ·➤

Assessment point

Can the children recognize how the author makes the story dramatic? **AF5/6**

- How do pages 40–43 set up our expectations for more stories about Team X?

Follow-up activities

Writing activities

- Write the email described on page 18. **(short writing task)**
- Write the end of mission report that Dani will file on the *NICE 'Mission Accomplished' report* Photocopy Master. **(longer writing task)**

Other literacy activities

- Enact some of the scenes using small world figures and film a short movie clip, adding voiceover. **(speaking and listening)**

Cross curricular and thematic opportunities

- Design and make a model transport system (like Hawkwing or one of the other X-crafts) based on an animal. **(DT)**
- Locate Patagonia on a map. Use atlases, books or the Internet to find out about its climate, coastline and oceans. **(Geography)**
- Use Google Earth to 'fly' from UK to Patagonia. Look at the coastline and identify a place where they think the research station might be. **(ICT, Geography)**

Meteorite

BY CHRIS POWLING

About this book

Team X arrives in California to find out about the Collector's plans to steal the M-35 meteorite only to discover that they are not needed – the precious meteorite is already protected by state-of-the-art security. But all is not as it seems. As the children test the security systems they find that the Collector is using fakery to get his prize.

Big themes: being flexible about responding to new challenges by changing plans, using and testing technology

Writing genres: narrative, a fact file and a briefing paper (non-chronological report)

You will need

- A snow globe (optional)
- *Vocabulary bookmark* Photocopy Master 18, *Teaching Handbook* for Year 5/P6
- *What are they thinking, feeling, saying?* Photocopy Master 27, *Teaching Handbook* for Year 5/P6
- *Chapter 5: planned events story map* Photocopy Master 3, *Teaching Handbook* for Year 5/P6
- *Secret Service memo* Photocopy Master 4, *Teaching Handbook* for Year 5/P6
- *NICE Mission Accomplished report* Photocopy Master 2, *Teaching Handbook* for Year 5/P6

	Literacy Framework objective	Target and assessment focus
Speaking, listening, group interaction and drama	○ Perform a scripted scene making use of dramatic conventions **4.2**	○ We can turn scenes in the story into a play script and perform it **AF2**
Reading	○ Compare different types of narrative and information texts and identify how they are structured **7.3**	○ We can recognize the language choices and text structures of different kinds of text **AF4**
	○ Explore how writers use language for comic and dramatic effects **7.5**	○ We can recognize and discuss how the author makes the story dramatic **AF5/6**
Writing	○ Experiment with different narrative forms and styles to write their own stories **9.2**	○ We can write a story in the form of a play script **AF1/2**

The following notes provide a structure for up to three guided/ group reading sessions. They can be used flexibly; you can focus on all three sessions, two or one session. The rest of the book can be read independently by the children between sessions.

Select appropriate activities from the suggestions below depending on whether the children will read during the session or whether they have read prior to the session. In this instance you will skip the 'During reading' section, although, you may wish to include the 'As you read' activity as part of your discussion of what they have read independently. In Session 1, children will read to the end of Chapter 2. Prior to Session 2, ensure the children have read Chapters 3–4 independently. In Session 2, they will read Chapter 5. Prior to Session 3, ensure they have read Chapter 6. In Session 3, they will read Chapter 7.

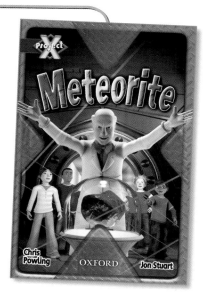

Session 1 (Chapters 1–2)

 ### Before reading

To activate prior knowledge and encourage reflection/prediction

- Show the children the snow globe and read page 3 together. Have the children already encountered the Collector in *Team X*? **(activating prior knowledge)**
- Then look at the destination information on pages 4–5. Ask the children to predict where this adventure will be set, who it will involve and what might happen to the meteorite. **(predicting)**
- Before children read independently, ask them to rehearse what they might do if they become stuck on a word or sentence. The range of possible strategies (such as rereading, reading on, using context, using phonic, syntactic and vocabulary knowledge) should be well established for most readers and only an occasional reminder should be necessary.

 ### During reading

- Ask the children to read to the end of Chapter 2.
- Stress the importance of comprehension, reminding the children to stop and take action if they are failing to understand the text, e.g. checking the meaning of a particular word or phrase, rereading more carefully, reading on to see if the meaning becomes clear, reading it aloud, discussing the passage with someone, etc.

- As they read, ask them to notice how the author uses language and layout to make the 'files' different from the narrative text.
- You could also ask them to note any new or unusual words and record these on their *Vocabulary bookmark* Photocopy Master.

· ·>

After reading

Returning to the text

- Ask the children:
  - o How has M-35 ended up at the HI-SCI Institute? **(recall)**
  - o Why do the children think the Collector will try to steal M-35? **(deducing, inferring and drawing conclusions)**
  - o What is the difference between a comet, a meteoroid and a meteorite? **(recall, summarizing)**

   Extension question: Why might an independent energy source be an important scientific discovery? **(deducing, inferring and drawing conclusions, building prior knowledge)**

The author's craft/Building vocabulary

- Share the words the children have recorded on their bookmarks. Point out any technical words from the 'files' and discuss why these words are in the files.
- Ask how the author uses language and layout to create the different types of text (narrative, non-chronological report) within Chapter 2.

· ·>

Building comprehension

- Freeze frame the scene at the end of Chapter 2 and ask each character what they are thinking and feeling at that point. The children could complete the *What are they thinking, feeling, saying?* Photocopy Master for the character they are portraying.

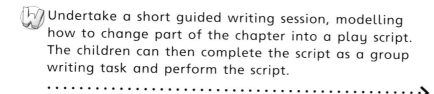Undertake a short guided writing session, modelling how to change part of the chapter into a play script. The children can then complete the script as a group writing task and perform the script.

. . . . >⟩

● Prior to Session 2, ensure the children have read Chapters 3 and 4 independently.

> **Assessment point**
>
> Can the children write the story in the form of a play script? AF1/2

> **Peer assessment point**
>
> Ask the children to assess each other's performance AF2

Session 2 (Chapter 5)

 Before reading

To review previously read text

● Ask the children to briefly recap the story to date. **(recall)**

To encourage prediction

● Look at the title of Chapter 5 and ask the children to predict what the characters are going to do. **(predicting)**

● Before children read independently, ask them to rehearse what they might do if they become stuck on a word or sentence.

 During reading

● Ask the children to read Chapter 5.

● Stress the importance of comprehension, reminding the children to stop and take action if they are failing to understand the text.

● As they read, ask them to notice the different problems that occur and how Team X adapt their plans to overcome these.

. . . . >⟩

> **Assessment point**
>
> Listen to individual children reading and make ongoing assessments on their approaches to tackling new words, their reading fluency and their understanding of the text. AF1

 After reading

Returning to the text

● Ask the children:

　o　What pieces of equipment help the characters find their way at the start of their journey? **(recall)**

o   Why do the characters end up on the wrong side of the door?
(recall, deducing, inferring and drawing conclusions)

o   Why is getting to M-35 described as being like an 'extremely hard assault course'? **(deducing, inferring and drawing conclusions)**

The author's craft

- Create a story map for Chapter 5. Draw it on top of the *Chapter 5: planned events story map* Photocopy Master. Ask the children to compare the planned and actual events.

- Then ask why the author makes the children's plans go wrong.

> **Assessment point**
>
> Can the children recognize and discuss how the author builds drama? **AF5/6**

· >

Building comprehension

- Invite the children to draw and label a picture of the security room from pages 34–35, using information from the text. **(visualizing)**

- Prior to Session 3, ensure the children have read Chapter 6 independently.

Session 3 (Chapter 7)

Before reading

To review previously read text

- Ask the children to tell you what has happened so far. **(recall)**
- What do they think the outcome will be? **(predicting)**
- Before children read independently, ask them to rehearse what they might do if they become stuck on a word or sentence.

During reading

- Ask them to read from Chapter 7 to the end of the story.

- Stress the importance of comprehension, reminding the children to stop and take action if they are failing to understand the text.

- As they read, ask them to reflect on their feelings about the story. **(personal response)**

> **Assessment point**
>
> Listen to pairs of children reading to each other and make ongoing assessments on their reading fluency. **AF1**

· >

 **After reading**

Returning to the text
- Ask the children which sections they particularly liked/didn't like. **(personal response, including adopting a critical stance)**

Building comprehension
- Ask the children to complete a storyboard, summarizing the final chapter in twelve frames. **(visualizing, determining importance, summarizing)**

Building vocabulary
- Share the words the children have recorded on their bookmarks. Look at them in context and check children understand their meaning.

Follow-up activities

Writing activities
- Create an MI5 agent alert memo, regarding the Collector, using the *Secret Service memo* Photocopy Master. **(short writing task)**
- Write the end of mission report that Dani will file on the *NICE 'Mission Accomplished' report* Photocopy Master. **(longer writing task)**

Other literacy activities
- The children could enact further scenes from the story. **(speaking and listening)**

Cross-curricular and thematic opportunities
- Create a map of a complex building. Write the instructions to get from point A to point B in the building using coordinates and turning instructions, e.g. 'turn 90 degrees clockwise, move to coordinates x,3'. Children invite a partner to follow the instructions. **(Maths)**
- Look at comets, meteorites, night skies in a range of media, e.g. in photographs, Halley's comet in the Bayeaux Tapestry, Van Gogh's *Cornfield on a starry night*. Use wax crayons and black/dark blue paint to produce wax resist paintings of meteorites, comets, etc. in the night sky. **(Art and design)**
- Make a simple burglar alarm that buzzes when pressure is applied to a spot (using electric circuits/contact points). **(DT, Science)**

Crack the Code

BY JOHN MALAM

About this book

Codes and ciphers have been used for thousands of years. This non-fiction book gives examples of different codes and ciphers and shows how they have been used throughout history.

Big themes: keeping secrets and turning messages into codes

Writing genres: non-chronological reports, instructions, factual narrative/recounts, explanations

You will need

- Two or three cards of each of these questions words: *Who, What, When, Where, Why, How*
- *Alberti Cipher disc* Photocopy Master 5, *Teaching Handbook* for Year 5/P6
- *Newspaper report frame* Photocopy Master 15, *Teaching Handbook* for Year 5/P6.

	Literacy Framework objective	Target and assessment focus
Speaking, listening, group interaction, and drama	○ Use and explore different question types and different ways words are used, including in formal and informal contexts 1.3	○ We can ask a range of questions **AF2**
Reading	○ Make notes on and use evidence from across a text to explain events or ideas 7.1	○ We can track ideas and information across a book **AF2**
	○ Compare different types of narrative and information texts and identify how they are structured 7.3	○ We can identify the features of different text types and understand how this relates to their audience and purpose **AF4/6**
	○ Distinguish between everyday use of words and their subject-specific use 7.4	○ We can explain and comment on specific words and their uses **AF5**
Writing	○ Create multi-layered texts, including use of hyperlinks and linked web pages 9.5	○ We can create an ICT text which is appropriate to the reader and purpose **AF2**

The following notes provide a structure for up to three guided/ group reading sessions. They can be used flexibly; you can focus on all three sessions, two or one session. The rest of the book can be read independently by the children between sessions.

Select appropriate activities from the suggestions below depending on whether the children will read during the session or whether they have read prior to the session. In this instance you will skip the 'During reading' section, although, you may wish to include the 'As you read' activity as part of your discussion of what they have read independently. In Session 1, children will read sections up to page 7. In Session 2, they will choose a section between pages 12–21. In Session 3, they will read page 22 together, and then a further section of their own choosing. Sections not read in guided/group reading sessions should be read independently.

Session I (pages 2–7)

 Before reading

To activate prior knowledge

- Look at the front cover and discuss the title. Talk about why codes need to be 'cracked'.
- Read pages 2 and 3 together and ensure the children understand the difference between a code and a cipher. Discuss any examples they know of codes and ciphers being used for examples in books or films. **(activating and building on prior knowledge)**
- Before children read independently, ask them to rehearse what they might do if they become stuck on a word or sentence. The range of possible strategies (such as rereading, reading on, using context, using phonic, syntactic and vocabulary knowledge) should be well established for most readers and only an occasional reminder should be necessary.

 During reading

- Ask the children to reread pages 2 and 3 and then to the end of page 7.

- Stress the importance of comprehension, reminding the children to stop and take action if they are failing to understand the text, e.g. checking the meaning of a particular word or phrase, rereading more carefully, reading on to see if the meaning becomes clear, reading it aloud, discussing the passage with someone, etc.

- As they read, ask them to note words that are new, interesting or puzzling.

Assessment point

Listen to individual children reading and make ongoing assessments on their approaches to tackling new words, their reading fluency and their understanding of the text. **AF1**

· ·>

 After reading

Returning to the text

- Ask the children to create some questions to ask each other concerning the information they have just read.

- Place the question cards face down. Ask each child to pick two or three cards. Going through the pages they have read, ask them to frame some questions beginning with the question words they hold. The rest of the group will answer the questions. Encourage them to ask a range of questions – some that need simple recall, others that require inference and synthesis, e.g. 'Can you make up a question where the answer is right there in the text/is given as clues in the text/needs you to put information together?' **(synthesizing, deducing, inferring and drawing conclusions)**

· ·>

Assessment point

Can the children ask a range of questions? **AF2**

The author's craft

- Look at pages 2 and 3 and point out the features of an explanation text; in this case, an opening general explanation of why it is needed or a statement of the problem (need to keep things private), definitions of code/cipher, explanation of the process of making a code/cipher with detailed examples.

· ·>

Building comprehension

- Check that children understand the explanation of the five-by-five cipher on pages 6 and 7, by getting them to complete one. **(recall, other sensory responses)**

Assessment point

Can the children identify the features of the text type and understand how it relates to the audience and purpose? **AF4/6**

- Prior to Session 2, you might like the children to read pages 8–11 independently.

Session 2 (pages 12–21)

 Before reading

To review previously read text/preview new text
- Ask the children to share any further information they recall from their independent reading about codes and ciphers. **(recall)**
- Quickly flick through pages 12–21 to get an overview of the contents.
- Before children read independently, ask them to rehearse what they might do if they become stuck on a word or sentence.

 During reading

- Ask the children to read on, selecting those pages that most interest them. Tell them how long they will have to read independently so they can plan their reading.
- Stress the importance of comprehension, reminding the children to stop and take action if they are failing to understand the text.
- As they read, explain that they will each tell the group two or three facts they found most interesting in the sections they select to read and why.

> **Assessment point**
>
> Listen to individual children reading and make ongoing assessments on their approaches to tackling new words, their reading fluency and their understanding of the text. **AF1**

· >

 After reading

Returning to the text
- Ask the children to share some of the facts that interested them.

The author's craft
- Look at the instructions for making a cipher disc on pages 16 and 17. Revise the structure and language features of instructions (list of what is needed, step-by-step commands, explanation of use).

> **Assessment point**
>
> Can the children identify the features of the text type and understand how it relates to the audience and purpose? **AF4/6**

· >

Building comprehension

- Check that children understand the instructions by asking them to make the Alberti cipher disc, using the *Alberti Cipher disc* Photocopy Master, and then decoding the message on page 17. **(recall, other sensory responses)**

Session 3 (pages 22–30)

 Before reading

To review previously read text

- Ask the children to recap on information from their reading. **(recall)**

To build vocabulary

- Introduce the word 'steganography' (p.22). Ask the children to skim the whole text together as far as page 22 and collect some of the vocabulary around codes and ciphers such as 'Morse', 'operator', 'cipher disc', 'substitution'. Discuss what they mean and their subject-specific and more general uses. For example, what does it mean to describe someone as a cipher? How is a Morse code operator different from/the same as a machine operator?

⋯⋯⋯⋯⋯⋯⋯⋯⋯⋯⋯⋯⋯⋯⋯⋯⋯⋯⋯⋯>

> **Assessment point**
>
> Can the children explain and comment on specific words and their uses? AF5

- Read page 22 together and discuss the many different ways code/ciphers can be hidden.

- Before children read independently, ask them to rehearse what they might do if they become stuck on a word or sentence.

 During reading

- Ask the children to read a further section of their own choosing independently. Ask them to be prepared to give a summary of what they have read.

- Stress the importance of comprehension, reminding the children to stop and take action if they are failing to understand the text.

⋯⋯⋯⋯⋯⋯⋯⋯⋯⋯⋯⋯⋯⋯⋯⋯⋯⋯⋯⋯>

> **Assessment point**
>
> Listen to individual children reading and make ongoing assessments on their approaches to tackling new words, their reading fluency and their understanding of the text. AF1

After reading

Returning to the text/Building comprehension

- Ask each child to give a brief oral summary of what they have read. **(recall, summarizing, determining importance)**
- Model making brief summary notes as they talk, using page numbers and key points.

Extension activity: Give pairs of children a topic, or allow them to select one that interests them: in particular, egg substitution ciphers, wartime codes, famous inventors of codes. Ask them to go back over the whole book making notes on this topic.

Self assessment point

Ask the children to check whether they have tracked information from across the books. AF2

Follow-up activities

Writing activities

- Ask the children to use their notes from the previous activity to write a brief ICT based report, adding visual information and combining them to make a hyperlinked PowerPoint presentation on codes and ciphers. **(short writing task)**
- Use the *Newspaper report frame* Photocopy Master to create an news item about one of the stories in the book, e.g. Mary Queen of Scots, finding the Rosetta stone, looking for the Beale treasure, etc. **(short writing task)**
- Make up a story about someone who finds a coded message and the adventure that it leads to. **(longer writing task)**

Other literacy activities

- Role play a scenario as a Morse code operator typing out an urgent/dramatic message. **(speaking and listening)**

Cross-curricular and thematic opportunities.

- Try out the semaphore KS2 resources from http://www.bletchleypark.org.uk/edu/teachers/ccresources.rhtm **(Maths)**
- Create a code and ciphers ICT based quiz. For an example, see http://library.thinkquest.org/J0112850/codesquiz.htm **(ICT)**
- Research symbols in heraldry and design a personal coat of arms. **(History, Art and design)**

The Secret Diary of Danny Grower

BY JOANNA NADIN

About this book

Danny finds a man who he thinks is a missing film star hiding in his Nan's shed. Danny agrees to help him remain hidden. But things are not what they seem. As Danny realizes he must take action, he discovers the strength of his family when he needs their help.

Big themes: family relationships, celebrity culture, jumping to conclusions

Writing genres: humorous writing, personal diary entries, postcards, lists, newspaper reports and magazine articles

You will need

- *What are they thinking, feeling, saying?* Photocopy Master 27, *Teaching Handbook* for Year 5/P6
- *Story planning frame* Photocopy Master 14, *Teaching Handbook* for Year 5/P6
- 3rd person story, e.g. fairy tale

	Literacy Framework objective	Target and assessment focus
Speaking, listening, group interaction and drama	○ Tell a story using notes designed to cue techniques, such as repetition, recap and humour 1.1	○ We can retell a story using humour to engage our listeners **AF2**
Reading	○ Explore how writers use language for comic and dramatic effects 7.5	○ We can recognize and discuss how the author makes a story funny **AF5/6**
	○ Compare the usefulness of techniques such as visualization, prediction and empathy in exploring the meaning of texts 8.2	○ We can use empathy to explore how a character feels **AF3**
Writing	○ Experiment with different narrative forms and styles to write their own stories 9.2	○ We can write a story in the form of diary entries **AF1/2**

The following notes provide a structure for up to three guided/group reading sessions. They can be used flexibly; you can focus on all three sessions, two or one session. The rest of the book can be read independently by the children between sessions.

Select appropriate activities from the suggestions below depending on whether the children will read during the session or whether they have read prior to the session. In this instance you will skip the 'During reading' section, although, you may wish to include the 'As you read' activity as part of your discussion of what they have read independently. In Session 1, children will read up to page 14. Prior to Session 2, ensure they have read pages 15–24 independently. In Session 2, they will read pages 25–33. Prior to Session 3, ensure they have read pages 33–45 independently. In Session 3 they will read pages 46–55.

Session 1 (pages 3–14)

 Before reading

To activate prior knowledge and encourage reflection/prediction

- Ask the children to talk about diaries – what they are and their experience of using and reading them. Talk about the different function of diaries. **(activating and building prior knowledge)**
- Before children read independently, ask them to rehearse what they might do if they become stuck on a word or sentence. The range of possible strategies (such as rereading, reading on, using context, using phonic, syntactic and vocabulary knowledge) should be well established for most readers and only an occasional reminder should be necessary.

 During reading

- Ask the children to read to the end of page 14.
- Stress the importance of comprehension, reminding the children to stop and take action if they are failing to understand the text, e.g. checking the meaning of a particular word or phrase, rereading more carefully, reading on to see if the meaning becomes clear, reading it aloud, discussing the passage with someone, etc.
- As they read, ask them to look out for information and clues to Danny's and his family and friends' personalities.

Assessment point

Listen to individual children reading and make ongoing assessments on their approaches to tackling new words, their reading fluency and their understanding of the text. AF1

After reading

Returning to the text

- Ask the children:

  o Why has Danny got nobody to play with at the moment? **(deducing, inferring and drawing conclusions)**

  o What details can you give about Danny's family (with reference to the text)? **(recall, deducing, inferring and drawing conclusions)**

  o What things show that Danny is obsessed with Kurt Gold/Jack Brown (with reference to the text)? **(recall, synthesizing, deducing, inferring and drawing conclusions)**

  Extension question: Why does Danny think there might be a money problem in the family? What is his evidence for that interpretation? **(synthesizing, deducing, inferring and drawing conclusions)**

The author's craft

- Why do they think the author is showing us that Danny has nothing exciting to do/write about?
- Ask the children to find examples of places where the author uses humorous phrases or humorous description of incidents.

· ·>

Assessment point

Do the children recognize how the author uses humour? Can they discuss the impact of this? AF5/6

Building comprehension

- Role play the scene in which Danny's parents confront Marcie with her phone bill.
- Ask them to consider the action from the point of view of their character and to bring out Marcie's exaggerated (teenage) actions/responses. Freeze frame the scene at the point at which Mum says "So sue me". Ask each character to say what they are thinking and feeling at that point. **(personal response, including adopting a critical response, empathizing)**
- Ask the children to complete the grid on the *What are they thinking, feeling, saying?* Photocopy Master for one of the characters at that point in the story. **(adopting a critical stance, empathizing)**

· ·>

Assessment point

Do the children realize how empathy helps them to understand a character? AF3

- Prior to Session 2, ensure the children have read pages 15–24 independently.

Session 2 (pages 25–33)

 Before reading

To review previously read text and encourage prediction
- Ask the children to briefly recap the story. **(recall)**
- Discuss what they know about Kurt Gold. Why does Danny think he is Kurt Gold and why is he helping him? Do the children think it is Kurt Gold. Why or why not? **(predicting)**
- Before children read independently, ask them to rehearse what they might do if they become stuck on a word or sentence.

 During reading

- Ask the children to read to the end of page 33.
- Stress the importance of comprehension, reminding the children to stop and take action if they are failing to understand the text.
- As they read, ask them to look for evidence of why Danny is willing to believe the man in the shed is Kurt Gold.

··>

 After reading

Returning to the text
- Ask the children:
  - o What items of food did Danny give to the man? **(recall)**
  - o How does Danny try to stop his mum, Nan and Marcie from becoming suspicious? Is he successful? **(recall, deducing, inferring and drawing conclusions)**
  - **Extension question:** Why did 'Kurt' laugh when Danny said 'you got it'? **(deducing, inferring and drawing conclusions)**

> **Assessment point**
>
> Listen to individual children reading and make ongoing assessments on their approaches to tackling new words, their reading fluency and their understanding of the text. AF1

The author's craft

- Ask the children to identify incidents and phrases that are funny. How does Danny's telling of these add to the humour?
- Allow the children time, in pairs, to choose a funny incident in the story to retell. Ask them to perform these to the group. **(visualizing and other sensory responses)**

· ·>

- Prior to Session 3, ensure the children have read pages 34–45 independently.

Session 3 (pages 46–55)

Before reading

To review previously read text and encourage prediction

- Ask the children to tell you what has happened so far. Were they surprised to find the parcel was the missing book manuscript? **(personal response)**
- What do they think Danny and Marcie should do? What do they think they will do? **(predicting)**
- Before reading independently, ask them to rehearse what they might do if they become stuck on a word or sentence.

During reading

- Ask the children to pair up and read pages 46–50 aloud to each other, taking it in turns to read a page. As they read, ask them to show their understanding of the characters' actions and emotions in the way they use their voice.
- Stress the importance of comprehension, reminding the children to stop and take action if they are failing to understand the text.
- Then children should read to the end of the story silently to themselves.

· ·>

After reading

Returning to the text

● Ask the children:

    ○   How did Danny know the man was not Kurt? **(synthesizing)**

    ○   Do you agree with Nan's view about secrets (p.54)? **(personal response, including adopting a critical stance)**

 Extension question: Why and in what ways does the newspaper account differ from the account in Danny's diary? **(deducing, inferring and drawing conclusions, adopting a critical stance)**

The author's craft

● Discuss the features of diary writing demonstrated in the book, e.g. Ist person, personal viewpoint, immediacy of action, inclusion of emotions, reactions, speculations as well as events.

Ask the children to rewrite a well known fairy tale such as 'Red Riding Hood' into a Ist person diary account written by one of the participants.

> **Assessment point**
>
> Can the children write a story in the form of diary entries, using appropriate features of the diary genre? AF1/2

• •➔

Follow-up activities

Writing activities

● Make up a story about finding something in a shed that initially the children keep secret but finally reveal. They can use the *Story planning frame* Photocopy Master to help them. **(longer writing task)**

● Change sections of the book from Ist person into 3rd person and discuss the effect. **(short writing task)**

● Write a brief email from Danny to his friend Zach summarizing what happened to him while Zach was away. **(short writing task)**

Other literacy activities

● Turn the story into a play script and enact it. **(drama)**

Cross-curricular and thematic opportunities

● Create a poster for one of the Jack Brown films or a book cover for the Jack Brown novel. **(Art and design)**

● Discuss when it is good to keep a secret, when it is dangerous to keep a secret and what to do if someone asks you to keep secret something you think should be revealed. **(PSHE)**

The Spy's Secret Handbook

BY JANE PENROSE

About this book

What skills do you really need to be a spy? In this guide, children will read about the skills spies use and learn how to acquire them. They will also find out about successful spies and spying operations.

Big themes: methods and skills of spying and government protection

Writing genres: job advertisement, non-chronological reports, instructions, explanations, factual narrative/recount

You will need

- Two or three cards of each of these question words: *Who, What, When, Where, Why, How*
- *Spies mind map* Photocopy Master 6, *Teaching Handbook for Year 5/P6*, enlarged to A3 size if possible

	Literacy Framework objective	Target and assessment focus
Speaking, listening, group interaction, and drama	○ Use and explore different question types and different ways words are used, including in formal and informal contexts **1.3**	○ We can ask a range of questions **AF2**
Reading	○ Make notes on and use evidence from across a text to explain events or ideas **7.1**	○ We can track ideas and information across the book **AF2**
	○ Compare different types of narrative and information texts and identify how they are structured **7.3**	○ We can identify the features of different text types and understand how this relates to their audience and purpose **AF4/6**
	○ Distinguish between everyday use of words and their subject-specific use **7.4**	○ We can explain and comment on specific words and their uses **AF5**
Writing	○ Create multi-layered texts, including use of hyperlinks and linked web pages **9.5**	○ We can create an ICT based handbook which is appropriate to the reader and purpose **AF2**

The following notes provide a structure for up to three guided/group reading sessions. They can be used flexibly; you can focus on all three sessions, two or one session. The rest of the book can be read independently by the children between sessions.

Select appropriate activities from the suggestions below depending on whether the children will read during the session or whether they have read prior to the session. In this instance you will skip the 'During reading' section, although, you may wish to include the 'As you read' activity as part of your discussion of what they have read independently. In Session 1, children will read up to page 9. In Session 2, they will choose a section between pages 16–25. In Session 3, they will read pages 26–29. Sections not read in guided/group reading sessions should be read independently.

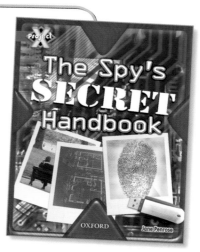

Session 1 (pages 2–9)

 Before reading

To activate prior knowledge

- Ask the children to record what they know about spying on the *Spies mind map* Photocopy Master. **(activating prior knowledge)**
- Before children read independently, ask them to rehearse what they might do if they become stuck on a word or sentence. The range of possible strategies (such as rereading, reading on, using context, using phonic, syntactic and vocabulary knowledge) should be well established for most readers and only an occasional reminder should be necessary.

 During reading

- Ask the children to read up to the end of page 9.
- Stress the importance of comprehension, reminding the children to stop and take action if they are failing to understand the text e.g. checking the meaning of a word or phrase, rereading more carefully, reading on to see if the meaning becomes clear, reading it aloud, discussing the passage with someone, etc).
- As they read, ask them to mentally note further important facts about spying.

> **Assessment point**
>
> Listen to individual children reading and make ongoing assessments on their approaches to tackling new words, their reading fluency and their understanding of the text. AF1

After reading

Returning to the text

● Ask the children to create some questions to ask each other about the information they have read, using the question cards. Encourage them to ask a range of questions – some questions that need simple recall and others that need inference and synthesis. **(questioning)**

· ·>

Building comprehension

● Ask the children, in pairs, to enact 'the brush pass' or 'the switch' from pages 8–9. **(visualizing and other sensory responses)**

● Ask the children to list the gadgets on pages 12–15 to create a catalogue. Then ask them to skim the whole book from the beginning and list further gadgets, adding page references. **(summarizing)**

· ·>

● Allow the children time to add notes to their *Spies mind map* Photocopy Master and to add further notes when reading independently.

● Prior to Session 2, you might like children to read pages 10–15 independently.

Session 2 (pages 16–25)

 Before reading

To review previously read text

● Ask the children to share the information from their *Spies mind map*.

● Before children read independently, ask them to rehearse what they might do if they become stuck on a word or sentence.

 During reading

● Ask the children to read pages 16–25.

● Stress the importance of comprehension, reminding the children to stop and take action if they are failing to understand the text.

- As they read, explain that they will each tell the group the two or three facts they found most interesting.

....>

 After reading

Returning to the text

- Ask the children to share some of the facts that interested them. **(recall, summarizing)**

The author's craft

- Look at the introductory paragraph on bugging on page 18. Revise the structure and language features of non-chronological reports (opening topic sentence, followed by details and examples).

....>

Session 3 (pages 26–29)

 Before reading

To review previously read text

- Ask the children to tell you what they have added to their mind maps.

To build vocabulary

- Quickly skim the text together and collect some of the spy speak vocadulary (in italics). Look at the spy speak chart on page 30. Discuss the subject-specific and general meanings of some of the terms, e.g. *cobbler*, *burned*, *naked*. Talk about why professions develop specialist vocabulary.

....>

- Before children read independently, ask them to rehearse what they might do if they become stuck on a word or sentence.

 During reading

- Ask the children to read pages 26–29.

> **Assessment point**
>
> Listen to pairs of children reading to each other and make ongoing assessments on their fluency. AF1

> **Assessment point**
>
> Can the children identify the features of this text type? AF4/6

> **Assessment point**
>
> Can the children explain and comment on specific words and their uses? AF5

- Stress the importance of comprehension, reminding the children to stop and take action if they are failing to understand the text.
- As they read, ask them to note further important facts about spying.

· ·>

 After reading

Returning to the text

- Ask the children:
    - o   What is a double agent? **(recall)**
    - o   What is a triple agent? **(recall)**
    - Extension question: How, why and by whom was Markov killed? **(recall, deducing, inferring and drawing conclusions)**

Building comprehension

- Ask the children to complete their *Spies mind maps*. **(determining importance, summarizing)**

· ·>

Follow-up activities

Writing activities

- Create hyperlinked ICT based pages, using the *Spies mind map* notes. **(longer writing task)**
- Add some imaginary gadgets to the catalogue. **(short writing task)**

Cross-curricular and thematic opportunities.

- Create invisible messages using lemon juice, lime juice and vinegar. Which is most successful? **(Science)**
- Identify suitable dead drop locations within the school grounds. Draw a scale plan of the grounds (e.g. I metre = I square) on squared paper. Identify the coordinates for the dead drop. Give the coordinates and scale map to another child for them to try to locate the dead drops by plotting the coordinates. **(Maths, Geography)**